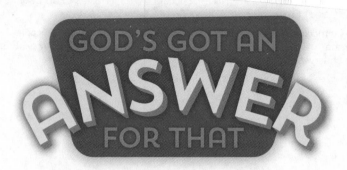

DEVOTIONAL

JON NAPPA
WITH SUZANNE HADLEY GOSSELIN

HARVEST HOUSE PUBLISHERS
EUGENE, OREGON

GOD'S GOT AN ANSWER FOR THAT DEVOTIONAL

Copyright © 2015 Jon Nappa
Published by Harvest House Publishers
Eugene, Oregon 97402
www.harvesthousepublishers.com

ISBN 978-0-7369-6123-3 (pbk.)
ISBN 978-0-7369-6124-0 (eBook)

Printed in the United States of America

14 15 16 17 18 19 20 21 22 23 / VP-JH / 10 9 8 7 6 5 4 3 2 1

Contents

Introduction

Hi! We're the Super Snoopers!
We're brothers who find antidotes
for life's problems in God's Word.

I'm Burt!

I'm Squirt!

We know life isn't always easy and kids run into lots of problems along the way. But guess what! For every problem, God's Word has an answer. You just have to know how to find it. And that's what this devotional is about. Each day, you'll look at a different problem and find the answer to that problem—right in God's Word! God always has the best solution and plan for your life.

For the advanced Truth Sleuth, we've included **extra**

snooping—these are verses to read that will help you understand the answer even better. And we'll be dropping by with extras, so look for us throughout the book. Don't forget to record your favorite promises from God's Word in the Truth Sleuth Log on page 89 as you go! See if YOU can discover even more answers from the Bible.

Never forget that when you have a problem, GOD'S GOT AN ANSWER FOR THAT!

Burt's a Truth Sleuth, Squirt's a Truth Sleuth, and you can be a Truth Sleuth too!

Keep Swimming

The PROBLEM: I am discouraged.

"I give up!"

Have you ever said those words? Struggling with a school subject, facing friend problems, or dealing with a physical challenge are just a few things that can make us feel like giving up.

Many years ago, a swimmer named Florence Chadwick attempted to swim from Catalina Island to the coastline of California, a 26-mile swim. The water was cold and partway through the swim, a thick fog covered the water, making it impossible to see land. After more than fifteen hours in the water, Florence became discouraged and gave up...not knowing that she was less than a mile from shore.

Not long after that, Florence tried again. This time there was also a fog, but she kept swimming, knowing the land was there. She swam so fast, she broke the men's record by two hours!

Find the ANTIDOTE

Read Romans 8:38-40 and make your own list of challenges that cannot separate you from God's love (examples: friend trouble, tests, sickness).

_____

_____

_____

Like Florence, we always have hope because God is our firm foundation and promises to help us overcome anything difficult we may face. He promises to always be with us and be our helper.

EXTRA SNOOPING: Read Hebrews 13:5-6.

No matter what challenges are making you feel discouraged today, God can help you conquer them. Keep swimming—your destination isn't as far away as you think.

I went swimming once. I was pretty good too!

You wore arm floats.

Sometimes you need a little help to conquer big challenges.

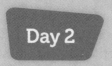

Battling a Bad Day

The PROBLEM: I am unhappy.

Tyler was having a bad day. First, he woke up half an hour late and had to rush to get ready for school. Then, his favorite cereal was gone after his sister ate the last bowl. He was halfway to the bus stop when he realized he'd forgotten his homework. And by the time he went home and returned to the bus stop, he'd missed the bus by a few minutes. Finally, Mom had to rearrange her schedule to drive him to school (which made her grumpy), and to make matters worse, Tyler had to collect a tardy note from the office when he got there.

Have you ever had a day like Tyler had, where everything seems to go wrong? Maybe your problems include trouble with friends, a bad grade on a test, or getting punished for having a bad attitude. Or perhaps you have BIGGER problems, like a family member is really sick, your dog ran away, or your parents are getting a divorce.

When problems come, they can make us feel very unhappy, sad, and even angry. Sometimes it seems like the problems are so big that they will never go away and we wonder if life will ever get better.

Find the ANTIDOTE

Read John 16:33 and write down what this verse says is the antidote (or cure) for problems.

_____

_____

_____

9

Jesus told His closest friends (called the disciples) that they shouldn't be surprised when they faced trouble. Problems are a natural part of life in this imperfect and sinful world. But Jesus reminded His friends of two things:

1. They could always find peace in Him.
2. He was more powerful than anything in the world, including their problems.

Write down the biggest problem you're facing right now:

_____

_____

_____

EXTRA SNOOPING: Look up these verses to discover three ways you can receive peace from Jesus:

Philippians 4:6
Isaiah 26:3
Psalm 119:165

(Hint: "Law" in this verse means God's Word.)

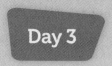

The Anger Bomb

The PROBLEM: I am angry.

Have you ever been so angry you felt like you were going to explode? It's kind of like when you shake a can of soda and then try to open it. All of the angry feelings build up inside until you open the can and everything explodes. Angry explosions are usually meant to scare or hurt others.

Angry feelings can come because of unfair circumstances, mistreatment by someone, or things not working out the way you had hoped. As a result, maybe you say unkind words to someone, yell, or throw something. Anger can be a big problem that affects you and others.

Find the ANTIDOTE

Read Ephesians 4:32. List two antidotes to anger that you read about:

1.

2.

When you concentrate on the opposites of anger—kindness, gentleness, and forgiveness—there's not as much room left in your life for anger to build up. Of course, there will be times when you get angry (even Jesus got angry). But the Bible has an answer for that too! It says, "In your anger do not sin" (Ephesians 4:26). If you struggle with anger that feels like a soda can about to explode, try these strategies to cool down:

Stay calm. Refuse to react in anger. Remove yourself from the situation and take a walk, count backward from 20, or punch a pillow. Once you have your anger under control, you can think more clearly about the situation and how you should respond.

Pray. This may be the most effective way to combat an angry explosion. When you feel angry feelings rising inside, take a time-out to pray for self-control and the right attitude. God will give you the perspective you need to not sin in your anger.

Don't let it build up. The second part of Ephesians 4:26 says, "Do not let the sun go down while you are still angry." It's important to get rid of anger as quickly as possible so it doesn't build up inside and get worse. God's enemy, Satan, would love to use your anger to get you into trouble, but don't let him!

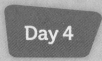

Stealing the Show

The PROBLEM: I'm a show-off.

Carter had a bad habit.

Every time someone did something cool, he had to top it. When a kid at the park crossed the monkey bars, Carter crossed them faster. When his younger brother said he could hold his breath for 20 seconds, Carter held his for 40. And when his friend Derrick told him about his family's summer road trip to Ohio, Carter bragged about his family's trip to a cool theme park.

Pretty soon Carter noticed that people didn't want to play with him or talk to him. One day, a kid at school muttered, "Carter, you're such a show-off!"

Showing off to gain attention or make yourself look better than others is a common problem. All people like to be recognized and feel good about themselves. But nobody likes to be around a show-off. How do you feel when, instead of noticing your accomplishment, your friend tries to top it? Think of how others feel when you do the same.

Find the ANTIDOTE

Read Romans 12:3. What is "sober judgment"? (Use a dictionary or Bible notes if you need to.)

God's Word encourages us to keep an accurate view of ourselves at all times. We don't have to show off our abilities to prove we are important; God says we already are important because He created us, loves us, and sent His Son to die for our sins. Others are important too. That's why we shouldn't think too highly of ourselves—or be prideful.

Next time you're tempted to show off, try focusing on the other person instead. Tell her, "good job," or ask him to tell you more about his cool trip. Then smile and remember what truly makes you important.

Day 5

Mine, Mine, Mine!

The PROBLEM: I am selfish.

Not long ago, somebody came up with a list of "property laws" for toddlers. Here are some of them:

1. If I like it, it's mine.
2. If it's in my hand, it's mine.
3. If I can take it from you, it's mine.
4. If I had it a little while ago, it's mine.
5. If it looks like mine, it's mine.
6. If I saw it first, it's mine.
7. If you put it down, it automatically becomes mine.
8. If it's broken, it's yours.

If you have a little brother or sister between the ages of one and three, this list probably sounds familiar. Unfortunately, some people never mature past the thinking of a toddler when it comes to their stuff. Maybe they hoard their money and possessions—not sharing with others. Or they may even try to take things from others just so they can have more. Selfishness is a BIG problem and one that everyone struggles with.

Find the ANTIDOTE

Read Philippians 2:3-5. How can you look out for the interests of others? Who set the perfect example of doing this?

_____

_____

_____

     Have you ever heard the phrase, "He's just looking out for number one!" That describes a person who does everything to make himself happy without thinking of others. Without Jesus living inside us and helping us to care about the needs of other people, our natural tendency is to just look out for ourselves. But a big part of being a Christian is getting rid of our selfishness and caring about God and other people.

List a few ways you can put others first this week:

My parents:

_____

_____

My friends:

_____

_____

My siblings:

_____

_____

Other people:

_____

_____

The Way to Obey

The PROBLEM: I don't want to obey.

Have you ever read a story or watched a movie about kids who were orphans or on their own? Maybe you wondered what it would be like to be on your own, making all of your own decisions without anyone telling you what to do.

No matter how much you love your mom and dad, there are probably times when you wish you didn't have to listen to them. You may even find yourself talking back or being disobedient.

The Bible tells us that's a problem! Find out why.

Find the ANTIDOTE

Read Proverbs 12:15. Including your parents, who are some other people it would be wise for you to listen to?

_____

_____

_____

Throughout your life, God will provide people who can give you wise advice. Parents have the special privilege of caring for you while you're a kid and helping you to grow up in the right way. Sometimes you may not like their advice or you may think you know better, but God promises special blessings for those who honor their parents.

19

EXTRA SNOOPING: Look up these verses and write down three good reasons for obeying your parents:

Exodus 20:12

_____

_____

Ephesians 6:1

_____

_____

Colossians 3:20

_____

_____

While there may be times where it seems like it would be fun to be on your own, thank God for giving you parents to love you, help you, and guide you.

Parents are a really big gift from God.

Dear old Mum and Dad taught us how to be truth sleuths in the first place!

Sticks and Stones

The PROBLEM: I say unkind words.

"Sticks and stones may break my bones, but words will never hurt me."

Maybe you've heard this saying before. The truth is, words can, and do, hurt. The words we say have the power to build others up or tear them down. That's why God tells us over and over to control our tongues and think carefully about what we say.

Have you noticed that you have a hard time being kind with your words? Maybe you're quick to make your brother feel bad about himself when he does something you don't like. You may have hurt a friend's feelings with your harsh words. Maybe you resort to name-calling when you become angry.

If unkind words are ruling you, there is a solution.

Find the ANTIDOTE

Read Luke 6:45. Copy down the last sentence of the verse here:

_____

_____

Unkind words come from a heart that is not in tune with Christ. When you're cultivating the right attitudes on the inside—by reading your Bible, praying, and seeking godly advice from others—your words will naturally follow. For example, if you're trying to love your sister the way Jesus tells you to, you're less likely to lash out at her with your words.

If you're spending time with the Lord and still struggling to keep control of your tongue, there are a few things you can concentrate on to transform your words from hurtful to helpful.

EXTRA SNOOPING: Look up these verses and write down the technique you find for controlling your tongue.

James 1:19

_____

_____

Psalm 34:13

_____

_____

Proverbs 15:1

_____

_____

Now draw a picture of yourself trying one of these techniques.

By allowing God to change your heart and letting good words flow out, what you say can heal, not hurt.

The Good Fight

The PROBLEM: I got into a fight with a friend.

Once there were two guys. They were good guys. In fact, they were missionaries who traveled around telling people about Jesus.

One day, these guys got into an argument. One of them wanted to take his cousin along on their next journey. The other guy didn't think his friend's cousin was responsible enough to go. In the end, the two missionaries couldn't agree so they parted ways, found new traveling buddies, and continued telling others about Jesus.

The two guys in the story were named Paul and Barnabas. Thankfully, the story of Paul and Barnabas is an extreme example; most fights between friends can be worked out.

EXTRA SNOOPING: You can read the story of Paul and Barnabas in Acts 15:36-40.

Find the ANTIDOTE

Read Matthew 18:15. What should you do to solve an argument?

_____

_____

_____

Here are some important things to remember about resolving conflicts:

First, keep it between the two of you. Getting a bunch of other people involved in your fight will only make things worse. It's best to go directly to the person who has hurt you and talk about what happened.

Stay calm and listen. When talking to your friend, listen calmly and try to understand why she's upset. When it is time for you to speak, talk about how you feel rather than accusing your friend. Say something like, "When you chose to go to Beth's party instead of going skating with me, I felt like you didn't want to spend time with me."

Choose peace and love. Paul, from the story above, also wrote: "If it is possible, as far as it depends on you, live at peace with everyone" (Romans 12:18). And 1 Peter 4:8 says: "Above all, love each other deeply, because love covers over a multitude of sins." Many times, having a desire to make things right is all it takes to end a fight.

Ask for help. If you and your friend can't come to an agreement, seek the advice of a parent, teacher, or another person who is wise in the Lord. They'll be able to help you and your friend end your fight and start your relationship fresh!

No Worries

The PROBLEM: I worry.

Someone once said that worry is like a rocking chair: "It gives you something to do but never gets you anywhere." When life gets stressful, worries about what *could happen* can take over. That's the problem: Many of the things we worry about never happen. And even if they do, being anxious didn't change anything. It probably made things worse.

There are lots of things you may worry about. Here are a few of them:

* Family problems
* School
* Friends
* Safety
* The future

What do you worry about? Make your own list here:

_____

_____

_____

Some people have a personality that naturally causes them to worry, while others are laid-back and can easily let go of concerns. No matter which personality you have, you can learn to let go of worries.

25

Find the ANTIDOTE

Read Philippians 4:6-7. What does this verse say to do *instead* of worry?

_____

_____

What does it say will happen when you do that?

_____

_____

Look at the list of worries you wrote down earlier. How can you use the solution found in Philippians 4:6-7 to set aside your anxiety in each situation?

Take some time right now to pray and give your worries over to God. Ask Him to give you peace and keep your heart and mind focused on Him instead of the "what ifs." When you do, you can get out of the worry rocking chair and start moving forward.

I kind of like rocking chairs.
I find them relaxing.

You just can't stay in
one forever.

Day 10

Behind-the-Scenes Ben

The PROBLEM: I feel like I don't matter.

Ben felt invisible. At school he was quiet. Around his friends, he rarely spoke up. And at church, where he sometimes served in the preschool class, he did the little jobs no one noticed, like filling water cups or picking up the trash. "Behind-the-scenes Ben," his dad liked to call him.

Even though Ben didn't mind the nickname, or even doing the little jobs, sometimes he wished people would notice him...like "Up-Front Fred." Fred played drums in the kids' band and people were always telling him how awesome he was. *Just once,* Ben thought, *it would be nice to feel important.*

Have you ever felt like Ben? Like your thoughts, opinions, and actions don't matter? Everyone feels that way sometimes, but the Bible reminds us of the truth.

Find the ANTIDOTE

Read 1 Corinthians 12:18-23. Why is every part (person) important in the Body of Christ?

_____

_____

_____

Make a list of some of the abilities God has given you that you can use to serve Him (examples: I'm good at art, I

27

encourage others through my words, I'm good at fixing things, I like to sing).

_____

_____

_____

Some people serve God in up-front roles that others notice. But other people serve in quiet ways that may never be noticed by others. The Bible says that both are important! In fact, God plans out who will serve in which roles. Jesus told His disciples that in God's kingdom, "The last will be first, and the first will be last" (Matthew 20:16). Just because you are unnoticed by people does not make you unimportant to God. Your role, no matter how small, matters to Him.

Look at the list you made above. Think of one way you can use your abilities to serve God (even if it's behind the scenes). Write it here:

_____

_____

Now pray and ask God to show you more ways—big and small—to get involved in what He is doing.

Big Fears

The PROBLEM: I am scared.

Were you ever afraid of a monster under your bed or the grumpy neighbor next door?

When you're younger, fears are pretty simple: monsters, the dark, spiders, big dogs. But as you grow older, the things you're afraid of become more complex: the bully at school, not being able to pass a test, natural disasters, getting sick, or someone you love dying. When you think about all of the things that could go wrong in your life, it's easy to begin to feel afraid.

Peter, one of Jesus's disciples, experienced this. One day, as he and the other disciples were sailing a boat across a lake, the waters and wind began tossing the boat around. Suddenly, they saw a man walking toward them on the water.

"It's a ghost!" Peter's friends called out. But it was Jesus.

Peter said, "Lord, if it's You, tell me to come to You on the water!" Jesus told him to come.

At that moment, Peter did something totally scary. He stepped out of the boat and onto the water. And he started walking—on the top of the water! But then he started focusing on things around him—the wind and the waves—and he began to sink!

"Lord, save me!" he cried. Jesus reached out, took Peter's hand, and brought him safely back to the boat.

Find the ANTIDOTE

Read Isaiah 41:13. What is one reason you don't have to be afraid?

_____

_____

What are a few of your fears? Make a list here.

_____

_____

_____

Just like Jesus had control over the wind and the waves and could easily save Peter, He also can take care of any situation that is making you afraid. When you keep your eyes on Him—instead of scary circumstances—you will feel peace and comfort. And with His help, you don't have to be afraid.

Take a minute to talk to God about your fears. Tell Him that you trust Him to care for you and help you with problems.

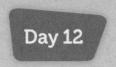

Day 12

Game Over

The PROBLEM: I play too many video games.

Brady knew he had a problem. All he wanted to do was play his favorite online video game. He woke up early to play a few minutes before school, and he stayed up late trying to beat just one more level. When he wasn't playing, he thought about the characters and new strategies he could use to beat the game. Soon he didn't have an interest in school, riding his bike, or even spending time with friends. *All* he thought about was his game.

One day, he heard his Sunday school teacher talk about the problem of being enslaved—or trapped—by something. Brady realized he was enslaved to his game. The time he spent playing and thinking about the game was taking away from other things he should be doing: homework, spending time with people, and serving God.

So Brady gave up his game. And he was serious about it. He unplugged his computer and asked his mom and dad to help him be accountable.

Find the ANTIDOTE

Read Proverbs 25:28 and draw a picture to illustrate the verse.

The Bible compares an uncontrolled person to a city whose walls are broken down. What is dangerous about this situation? A lack of self-control leaves you at risk for enemies to come in. You may think, *What's wrong with playing a video game?* And the answer may be *nothing*. But if you become addicted to a game, or anything else, you are allowing something besides Christ to rule your life.

And if you give in to little cravings as a kid, like too much

TV time, video games, or overeating, you may have a harder time avoiding more serious bad habits later on. The great news is, Jesus can free you from anything that is stealing your focus from Him.

EXTRA SNOOPING: Read John 8:36.

Brady quit his game for good and was able to start focusing on more important things, like his relationship with God and people. Instead of letting his walls get broken down, he started building them up.

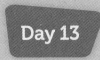

True or False

The PROBLEM: I didn't tell the truth.

Ellie was an exaggerator. When her mom asked if she'd cleaned her room, Ellie would say, "It's almost done!" when she'd only just made the bed. When her friend Lila asked what Ellie was doing for the weekend, Ellie would answer, "I'm going out on my uncle's boat, and we might even go waterskiing," when she knew they were only having a barbecue. And when her dad asked how long she'd been working on her homework, Ellie would say, "Two hours!" when she'd only been working for 45 minutes.

Exaggeration is a form of lying. Anything you say that is not 100 percent true is a lie. Some reasons you might lie are to avoid getting in trouble or to make yourself look better than you are. You may even be tempted to lie so you don't hurt someone's feelings with the truth. But there's a reason that it's never right to lie.

Find the ANTIDOTE

Read Proverbs 12:22. Look up the words *detest* and *delight* that you find in this verse. What does each word mean?

Detest _____

_____

Delight _____

_____

Telling the truth is a big deal to God. That's because God *is* truth. When you exaggerate here or there or tell a small lie that doesn't seem to matter, you may think it's not important. But lying is even mentioned in the Ten Commandments (Exodus 20:16)!

Telling the truth is a way of life. If you regularly speak only the truth, you will be a trustworthy person. If you regularly stretch the truth, you will have to tell more and more lies to cover up your dishonesty. That's why we delight God when we speak and live by the truth.

Telling the truth is the first rule of being a truth sleuth.

Yeah! Instead of getting caught in a web of lies, the truth will set you free!

Cheating Ways

The PROBLEM: I cheated.

Sarah had done it again.

She'd told herself that last time was the *last time,* but when she got stumped during the quiz she glanced over at Anna's paper. It was so easy to see her friend's answer. And once she saw it, she couldn't get it out of her mind. *Of course that's the right answer,* she thought. *And now that I remember, it's not really cheating...* Still, Sarah had a sick feeling in the pit of her stomach.

Have you ever been in the same situation as Sarah? The temptation to cheat can be a strong one. And sometimes it is *so* easy! Whether in sports or on schoolwork, cheating is about taking a sinful and dishonest shortcut to get what you want. You may feel pressure to get good grades or be liked by your teacher. Maybe you don't want to disappoint your parents or teammates with a poor performance. Or maybe you'd rather spend time doing other things...so you take a shortcut by cheating on a test instead of studying for it and succeeding the right way.

Whatever the reason for being tempted to cheat... cheating is never the right path.

Find the ANTIDOTE

Read Proverbs 10:9. How is cheating a "crooked path"?

_____

_____

So what if you *have* already cheated? It may be really hard, but you need to make things right. You should tell a parent or your teacher. If you have to confess what you've done, it may be embarrassing, but it will make it much harder to cheat the next time.

Even if you feel like you got away with cheating and nobody knows, God knows. Someone has said: "Integrity is doing the right thing even when no one is watching." Cheating chips away at your integrity and can damage your reputation, and more importantly, your character. The path of a cheater is never a safe path.

Pray and ask God to show you how to avoid dishonest ways and give you courage to confess any cheating you've already done. He can help you walk the secure path of integrity from now on!

Day 15

Wishing for More

The PROBLEM: I am not happy with what I have.

Anna frowned at the cardboard box in front of her. It was time to open up another box of hand-me-down clothes from her older sister, Mariah. It wasn't that Anna never got new things. She always got two new outfits for back-to-school and some new clothes at Christmas and on her birthday, but sometimes she wished *she* were the older sister so all of her things could be new.

She thought about her friend Nessa. Nessa's parents were both doctors and she could buy something new anytime she wanted. She had her own room and never had to wear hand-me-downs. *I wish I had all the money I wanted,* Anna thought. *Then I wouldn't have to wear Mariah's old clothes.*

Have you ever felt like Anna? When you compare what you have to what others have, do you feel like you got a bad deal? Maybe you wish you had more money, a bigger house, or more toys. The Bible has a lot to say about contentment.

Find the ANTIDOTE

Read the following verses and write each one in your own words.

Hebrews 13:5

_____

_____

_____

37

1 Timothy 6:8

_____

_____

_____

The first verse reminds us that there are things that are more important than money and stuff—the biggest one is having Jesus with us in EVERY circumstance. And the second verse says as long as our basic needs are met (food and clothing), we should be happy—or satisfied—with what we have. Answer these questions:

What is one thing you wish you had right now?

_____

Looking at your whole life—from now until you die—how important is that thing on a scale of 1 to 10?

_____

Will it matter in ten years? Five years? One year?
Make a list of some things God has provided for you. Write your list on a piece of paper and hang it somewhere you'll see it every day. Look at it often to remind yourself of things you *do* have. Pretty soon, you may forget about the things you don't.

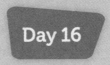

Day 16

Sibling Survival

The PROBLEM: I fight with my brother or sister.

Imagine if God gave you a friend to be with you your whole life. You'd grow up together, do many of the same activities, and know all of the same people. Whenever you felt like no one else could understand you, this friend would, because he or she had known you all along.

Would you like a friend like that? If you have a brother or sister, you already have one. *But wait,* you may be thinking, *my sister drives me crazy!* Or, *my brother and I fight all the time.* Fighting between brothers and sisters—known as "sibling rivalry"—is common, but that doesn't mean it has to ruin the special relationship God has for you.

Find the ANTIDOTE

Read Ephesians 4:31-32. Make a list of some of the ways this verse provides for getting along with your sibling:

_____

_____

_____

The Bible uses the example of brothers and sisters to tell us how we are to treat fellow Christians. God is our Father, and we are supposed to treat other believers like we are members of the same family. The Bible even says that you cannot love God if you do not love your brother or sister (1 John 4:20)! That's a good reason to be kind to them.

You may not always feel buddy-buddy with your sibling, but here are a few ways you can get along:

Communicate. If you're feeling upset with your brother or sister, try to have a calm conversation to work things out.

Show grace. Look for the best in your sibling instead of the worst. Notice the good things they do and point those out. For example, "Thanks for helping me unload the dishwasher, Ben. You made the job go a lot faster."

Have fun. Studies show that the closest siblings are those who have fun together and laugh a lot. Do something fun with your brother or sister: Play a game, make up a comedy routine, or plan a fun outing to the park.

We don't always get along perfectly, but we're glad that God made us brothers.

It's great to always have a friend to solve mysteries with!

Day 17

Go to Church

The PROBLEM: I don't feel like going to church.

"Church is boring."

"I'd rather sleep in."

"But I don't have any friends there."

Have you ever found yourself giving any of these excuses for not wanting to go to church? Joel admits the only reason he likes going to church is because of the delicious blueberry muffins his mom bakes every Sunday morning.

There are lots of reasons you may not feel like going to church (even if you know you should). Maybe there are other things you'd rather do. Maybe you don't feel like you fit in at church. Maybe reading the Bible and singing songs feels boring. Or perhaps you think, "I'm already a Christian, so why do I need to go to church anyway?"

Find the ANTIDOTE

Read Hebrews 10:25, then write the verse in your own words:

_____

_____

_____

The Bible warns us that there will be times when we don't feel like going to church, but we should go anyway. Church is the place where we learn more about God, worship Him, and receive encouragement from others who also believe. More than that, the *Church*—not the building, but all believers everywhere—is the platform Jesus uses to reach the world with His love and salvation! How exciting to get to be a part of the things Jesus is doing in the world.

If you've still got the church-blues, try these tips:

Treat church like a special event. The night before (or earlier in the day), set aside your Bible, offering, and the outfit you're planning to wear. (Maybe you can even talk your mom into making blueberry muffins!)

Be a friend. Take time to get to know at least one other person at church whom you can sit with and encourage.

Make it an all-week thing. Church doesn't have to be a Sunday-only thing. As you read your Bible during the week, write down questions you have for your Sunday school teacher or pastor. Consider attending a midweek program if your church offers one. Or volunteer with another ministry, like serving in the nursery.

Happy Helper

The PROBLEM: I don't know how to help others.

Lydia wondered how she could help. The nine-year-old had just heard about the terrible earthquake in Haiti that killed many people and left others without homes. "I didn't know Haiti existed before then," Lydia says. "It's such a poor country. It made me think about all the poor people who live in the world. I thought, *What if I was the one living in a one-room hut with dirt floors and the earthquake killed my family? That would be terrible.*"

Lydia did what she could to start. She prayed for Haiti each day. Soon she heard about an opportunity to raise money to build a playground for a school in Haiti. Lydia's parents helped her find a company that sold jewelry made by women in Haiti. Lydia hosted "jewelry parties" at her house and people began to tell their friends about what Lydia was doing. Soon she had raised $6,000—more than enough to build the playground!

Like Lydia, you may wonder how you can help others. You may feel like you can't do much because of your age or because you don't have a lot to give. But God's Word says differently.

Find the ANTIDOTE

Read Galatians 6:2. What do you think it means to "carry each other's burdens"?

_____

_____

When you notice that others are having a hard time, pray and ask God how you can help. Ask your parents too. Together you can find a way to help. It doesn't matter how old you are or how much money you have. God can use you to make a difference and help others!

On a warm January day, Lydia and her family stepped out of a car to visit the school in Haiti where the playground had been built. She ran full speed toward the playground. "Seeing it, I was so amazed I could cry, knowing God had used me to build it," she says.

Write down a person or people who may need your help:

_____

What are some ways you could help them?

_____

_____

_____

Take a few minutes to pray that God would give you the desire to help others and show you ways to do it.

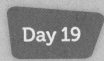

The Backtalk Trap

The PROBLEM: I argue with others.

Dylan always had to be right.

When his parents told him to do something, he always had a good reason for why he shouldn't have to. When his friends talked about their favorite comic characters, Dylan corrected them on the storylines. And when his brother told him it was his turn to feed the dog, Dylan argued that he did it last time.

Do you have a problem with arguing? Maybe, like Dylan, you always want to be right. Perhaps you don't like to be told what to do. Or maybe people say things that bother you and you feel a need to correct them.

Whatever the reason, arguing should not be a regular part of the Christian's life. Find out why.

Find the ANTIDOTE

Read Philippians 2:14-15. How many things are you supposed to do without arguing?

_____

What happens when you don't argue or complain?

_____

There are several types of arguing. Here are a few:

Fighting—an angry disagreement that may get physical.

Talking back—using words to challenge or correct an authority figure, such as a parent or teacher.

Bickering—arguing in an annoying way about things that aren't important.

Which type of arguing do you struggle with the most? No matter what form arguing takes, it keeps us from being the people God wants us to be. Because it's tempting to argue at times, those who don't bicker or fight stand out "like stars in the sky" and are a powerful example of how Christ changes lives.

Do Not Steal

The PROBLEM: I took something that wasn't mine.

Are you a thief?

You might say, "I've never robbed a bank or stolen someone's wallet." But have you ever taken *something* that wasn't yours—even something small? Maybe you took a dollar bill off of your dad's dresser. Maybe you filled your cup with soda at the fast-food restaurant when you ordered water. Or maybe you took something you wanted from the store.

If you're okay with taking small things that aren't yours, you've probably at least thought about taking bigger things. Stealing is a big problem that's even mentioned in the Ten Commandments (Exodus 20:15).

Find the ANTIDOTE

Read Ephesians 4:28. What are we told to do instead of stealing what we want?

_____

_____

_____

When you are a Christian, stealing is not an option. Instead of taking things from others, we're told to work hard for the things we have so that we can give to others. Sometimes you may be tempted to steal so you can have what you want right now. Or you may think you need the thing more than the person who owns it. But whatever excuse you make for stealing, it's never right to take what isn't yours.

Here are three things you can do when you're tempted to steal:

Ask permission. The person may be willing to lend you something or even give it to you.

Work and wait. When you want something, work to earn money so you can buy it.

Get away. If you're tempted to steal something no one will notice, walk away from the temptation.

JUST FOR FUN, see if you can match these "stealing" phrases with their meanings:

1. Steal a kiss	a. get a good price on something
2. Steal a base	b. to gain another person's love
3. Steal someone's heart	c. to draw all the attention to oneself
4. Get something for a steal	d. to smooch someone unexpectedly
5. Steal someone's thunder	e. lessen someone else's authority
6. Steal the show	f. to sneak from one base to another in baseball

Answers: 1. d.; 2. f.; 3. b.; 4. a.; 5. e.; 6. c.

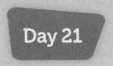

Pride Busters

The PROBLEM: I only do things my way.

Ava frowned. She and her friend Ella had decided to write a play to act out for their parents. But the two girls couldn't agree on the characters or storyline.

"I'll be the princess and you can be the evil queen," Ava said. "I played Cinderella in the school play, so I know what I'm doing."

"Why can't we be sister princesses?" Ella suggested. "We can ask my brother, Max, to be the evil prince."

Ava shook her head. "No, that won't work. Either I'm the *only* princess, or I'm not playing."

Do you see anything wrong with Ava's attitude? It's not unusual to have moments where you want to do things your own way. But thinking you're always right and others are wrong can lead to big problems.

Find the ANTIDOTE

Read Proverbs 3:7-8. What do you think this verse means?

_____

_____

_____

No person is right all the time. And if you think you are, you are putting yourself in a dangerous spot. Proverbs 16:18 says, "Pride goes before destruction, a haughty spirit before a fall."

Instead of an attitude that says "my way or the highway,"

seek to listen to the opinions of others and value their ideas. Everyone has something to contribute and you can learn from others just as they can learn from you.

For each of the following categories, write down a specific idea for your own life. (Example, "Next time I'm playing with my friend, I will offer to do something he wants to do.")

I need to:

Listen to advice

_____

_____

Go along with someone else's idea

_____

_____

Admit someone else is right and I am wrong

_____

_____

Use the list above as your pride-busting to-do list. You'll be a better friend and gain some valuable ideas from others in the process.

Working It

The PROBLEM: I don't do my work.

Take this quiz to find out what kind of worker you are.

1. When it's time to do chores, I...
- A. Dive right in so I can finish and do something fun.
- B. Do something else first, such as eat a snack or watch TV.
- C. Wait until my mom or dad forces me to do them.

2. When I have a homework assignment, I...
- A. Get started the first day I receive the assignment.
- B. Wait until the night before the homework is due to get working on it.
- C. Usually finish what I can on the way to school and sometimes don't complete assignments.

3. When I need to make money, I...
- A. Ask parents, friends, and neighbors if I can do some odd jobs to earn some cash.
- B. Empty my piggy bank and search under the couch cushions for change.
- C. Hope a tooth will fall out so the Tooth Fairy will bring me some money.

If you answered mostly A's, you're a hard worker who gets the job done. If you answered mostly B's, you do the minimum amount of work necessary. If you answered mostly C's, you avoid work as much as possible.

Find the ANTIDOTE

Read Colossians 3:23. How are we supposed to work?

_____

_____

_____

If you've ever felt like you didn't want to do your work, you're not alone! Everyone has moments when they'd rather do something else. But being a diligent worker—someone who works without giving up—is a way of serving God. He can use the work you accomplish to bless others and develop good character in you.

If you have a hard time getting serious about work, try these tips:

Get started right away. The longer you put work off, the harder it can be to get started.

Tackle bigger projects in pieces. Need to clean your room or do a science project? Break the job into smaller pieces and check each one off the list.

Make it fun. Play some music, munch on a healthy snack, or plan something fun for when the job is done.

Remember Who you're doing it for. When you're lacking motivation, remember that working hard is a way to honor God.

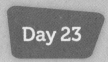

Day 23

When Life Is Hard

The PROBLEM: I think life is too hard.

Have you ever felt like life was too hard? Brendon has. That's because he was born with Cerebral Palsy, a condition that affects muscle coordination. Brendon can't walk and uses a wheelchair to get around. Having CP makes even simple daily tasks seem difficult. "I can't get dressed or brush my teeth by myself in the morning," he says.

Sometimes Brendon gets down when he thinks about the things he can't do, like run around and play baseball. When life feels hard, Brendon says he listens to worship music, spends time with friends, and remembers that God is always there to help.

Not long ago, Brendon demonstrated his faith in Christ by being baptized at his church. At first he was nervous about being in front of so many people. "The night before I was baptized, God told me, 'I've got this, friend!'" he says. Brendon knew he could face his fears with God by his side.

Life may be hard for Brendon, but he has this advice for other kids: "God is always there even though you can't see Him. Keep on fighting."

Find the ANTIDOTE

Read Philippians 4:13. What does this verse say you can do?

_____

_____

What gives you the ability to do it?

_____

_____

What are some things in your life that are making life seem hard right now? (Examples: a bully at school or a difficult test coming up.)

_____

_____

_____

Rewrite your list, beginning with the words "God can give me strength to..."

_____

_____

_____

Whatever challenges you may be facing, God can give you strength to get through them. He loves you and promises to give you help, courage, and protection every time you need it.

I admire Brendon's attitude!

Yeah, with God's help, he doesn't let the hard stuff get him down.

School Problems

The PROBLEM: I don't want to go to school.

"Why do I have to go to school?" Rylee pouted. "It's boring and I never learn anything anyway!"

Rylee's mom sighed. "You need an education because it will open doors for your future," she said.

"But I don't want to go," Rylee replied, tears filling her eyes.

What Rylee wasn't telling her mom was that she didn't have friends at school and some of the girls were mean. On top of that, she was having a hard time understanding math and was afraid she would get a bad grade.

Whether you attend public school, private school, or are homeschooled, you may feel the same as Rylee at times. Maybe you have a hard time fitting in with classmates or feel stressed about schoolwork. Maybe you're bored and wonder, "What's the point?" It may surprise you that education is God's idea.

Find the ANTIDOTE

Read Proverbs 18:15. How does this verse describe those who seek out knowledge?

_____

_____

Learning is important. At this time in your life, your whole job is to acquire knowledge! That's pretty cool, when you think about it. You can learn about anything you want to. School is one place that will help you learn and grow into the adult God wants you to be. Education will also give you more options for your future.

Make a list of some things you like about school:

_____

_____

_____

Focusing on the positives of learning can help you have a better attitude about school. Check out some solutions to common "school blues."

I'm bored. Talk to your parents and teacher to explain why you're bored. Maybe your teacher can offer you some extra projects to keep you busy and learning!

I'm stressed about schoolwork. Tell your parents about your worries and ask them to give you extra help in subjects you're struggling with. A little extra practice can make a big difference!

I don't have friends. Pray and ask God to provide you with a good friend. While you're waiting, be a friend to others by being kind and looking for ways to serve.

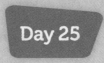

You Have the Wrong Idea

The PROBLEM: I feel misunderstood.

Misunderstandings happen. Even one wrong word can change someone's entire meaning. Check out these funny mistakes found in real church bulletins. (Can you identify what's wrong with each one?)

* Helpers are needed! Please sign up on the information sheep.

* Applications are now being accepted for two-year-old nursery workers.

* A worm welcome to all who have come today.

* Ushers will eat latecomers.

Yikes! It would be frightening to attend that last church. Instead of finding a seat, a visitor might become someone's meal!

Everyone feels misunderstood sometimes. Saying exactly what you mean isn't always easy to do. And a misunderstanding can lead to conflict and hurt feelings. Maybe you said or did something that unintentionally hurt another person, or maybe someone misjudged you. However the misunderstanding happened, it's important to correct it.

Find the ANTIDOTE

Read Matthew 5:23-24. What does this verse say you should do when a misunderstanding has occurred?

_____

_____

The very best way to handle a misunderstanding is to go directly to the person and explain your actions or what you intended to communicate or do. Help them understand what you really meant by your words or actions.

When Sophia was at summer camp, her counselor said it was time for the girls to get in their bunks for the night. Eager to help, Sophia switched off the light. "Turn the light back on now!" her counselor snapped. "It's time for our evening devotions."

Sophia turned the light back on but felt really sad. The next day, she explained to her counselor that she had been trying to help. Her counselor apologized for her harsh words and gave Sophia a hug.

Do you have a misunderstanding that needs to be cleared up? Go to the person and lovingly help them understand what you really meant. Draw a picture of the two of you having the conversation.

Day 26

The Great Tutu Mistake

The PROBLEM: I rush to judgment.

Not long ago a popular magazine published a picture of two women running a marathon wearing tutus and superhero T-shirts. The magazine made fun of the women, saying that the trend of dressing this way for competitive running was silly.

What the magazine didn't know was that one of the women in the picture had brain cancer and was wearing the costume as motivation and a show of support for others with cancer. Not only that, but the woman had a business making the tutus that had raised thousands of dollars to help young girls get healthy through exercise.

As you can imagine, the people who published the picture felt pretty embarrassed. The magazine made a statement saying: "If tutus make you run with a smile on your face or with a sense of purpose or community, then they are indeed worth wearing, for any race."

Sometimes we may be tempted to rush to judgment about others and say or do things that are unkind. Or maybe a situation makes us angry and we misjudge someone's motives. Rushing to judgment and acting on it is never a smart idea.

Find the ANTIDOTE

Read Proverbs 18:2. What factors might be necessary for you to understand a situation?

_____

_____

Have you ever shared your opinion and found out later you were wrong? Here are a few ways to be sure you understand before rushing to judgment:

Wait and listen. James 1:19 says we should be "Quick to listen, slow to speak and slow to become angry."

Find out the facts. If the magazine had asked the woman why she was wearing a tutu instead of jumping to conclusions, it would have saved itself a lot of embarrassment. Take time to check into all the facts before you form your opinion.

Pray. If something happens that angers you, it's always a good idea to check in with God. Ask Him to help you understand the situation or the motives of the person who hurt you.

Hurtful Words

The PROBLEM: I make fun of people.

Jenna sat on the edge of the table squirting ketchup on her hot dog.

"*Ew!* I can't believe you like hot dogs," Macy said rudely.

Some other girls laughed.

Zooey had been watching the whole thing. She felt bad for Jenna, but she also wanted Macy to like her. Before she could stop herself, the words slipped out: "Yeah, Jenna. Do you *know* what those things are made of? Gross!"

The other girls laughed even harder and Zooey felt great...for a few seconds.

That's when she saw the flash of sadness in Jenna's eyes. No one was ever nice to Jenna. She was weird and said odd things...and that made her an easy target for ridicule. Even though Zooey felt good being accepted, somewhere deep inside she was ashamed of her actions.

Find the ANTIDOTE

Read Genesis 1:27. Based on this verse, why should we treat other people with kindness?

_____

_____

No matter what a person looks like, the clothes they wear, how smart they are, how they talk, God created that person and loves him or her. That's a very good reason to respect everyone.

Jesus spoke about this very thing in Matthew 5:22 when

He said, "Anyone who says to a brother or sister, 'Raca,' is answerable to the court. And anyone who says, 'You fool!' will be in danger of the fire of hell."

Those words may sound a little harsh to us. *Raca* was a name that meant "empty," maybe a bit like calling someone "stupid." Obviously, it was a big deal to Jesus when people made fun of other people created in God's image.

Next time you're tempted to make fun of someone—even if you're just going along with the crowd—think twice. Remember that the person is created in God's image and loved by Him. Think of how God would treat that person and do the same.

The Bible compares the tongue to a raging fire—because words can be so destructive.

I think I'll go get a milkshake to put out the flames!

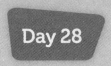

Bedtime Blues

The PROBLEM: I don't want to go to bed.

The time of day Grace dreaded most was here: bedtime. Her worries would begin just after dinner. As she cleared plates off the table, she thought about how she could delay bedtime or convince her mom to let her stay up a little later.

The problem was, once Grace was in bed with the lights off, she had a hard time falling asleep. Worries from the day would rush into her mind and make her feel anxious. It seemed she couldn't get her brain to shut down. The dark and quiet made her feel alone, and, at times, even afraid. Bedtime was the WORST time of day.

Maybe, like Grace, you don't like going to bed. Whether the reason is fear or a mind that just won't shut down, you may need a bedtime makeover.

Find the ANTIDOTE

Read Psalm 4:8. What reason does this verse give that we can we sleep in peace?

_____

_____

The Bible tells us we don't have to be afraid because God is our source of safety. He never sleeps and watches over us 24/7. If you're still having a hard time snoozing, make over your bedtime with these three ideas:

Wind down early. Try doing quiet activities 30 minutes

63

before lights-out. Spend some quiet time doing devotions, reading a book, writing in a journal, or drawing.

Follow the same routine. Studies show that we sleep better when we have a bedtime routine. For example: take a shower, put on pajamas, brush teeth, read, and pray. A routine prepares your body to sleep.

Put your focus on Jesus. Before bed, avoid scary TV shows or things that make you feel worried. Instead, end your day by reading a few Bible verses, listening to worship music, and talking to God. Invite your parents to pray with you for peaceful sleep.

My favorite teddy bear helps me go to sleep.

Isn't someone here a little old for that?

Oh, no, he's still a very young bear.

Wise Guy

The PROBLEM: I need wisdom.

The Bible tells us about a very special king named Solomon. One day, God appeared to Solomon and told him he could ask for anything. What an opportunity! If you could ask for anything, what would you choose? Solomon could have asked for riches or a long life or victory over his enemies. But he didn't ask for any of those things. As the ruler over a large number of people, Solomon had many important decisions to make every day. So although he could ask for *anything,* Solomon asked God for wisdom.

God granted his request and Solomon became the wisest king who ever lived. Rulers from surrounding nations came just to talk to the wise king. Solomon wrote the book of Proverbs, which is full of wise advice about life.

Wisdom is the ability to use one's knowledge or experience to make good decisions. Why is wisdom so valuable? Check out what King Solomon wrote in the Bible.

Find the ANTIDOTE

Read Proverbs 3:14-24. Make a list of the benefits of wisdom:

_____

_____

_____

You probably didn't even have room to write down *all of the ways* wisdom can help you. The bottom line is that wisdom leads to a good life and God is the One who gives wisdom.

What are some situations you might need wisdom for?

EXTRA SNOOPING: Read Proverbs 1:7.

The Bible says honoring the Lord is the start of wisdom. Whenever you're facing a hard decision, pray for wisdom and look to God's Word for answers! God loves to answer requests for wisdom, just like He did with Solomon.

Today I need wisdom to...

_____

_____

Looks Aren't Everything

The PROBLEM: I worry about how I look.

Sarah studied herself in the mirror. Her hair looked limp, more freckles seemed to be appearing on her nose each day, and her arms looked like two skinny, awkward branches. Sarah couldn't help but notice all of the ways her appearance didn't measure up to the "pretty girls."

Ethan was the smallest boy in his class. With a younger brother his same height, Ethan often felt embarrassed and self-conscious about his size.

Most people can think about things they would like to change about how they look. Maybe you wish to be skinnier or taller or have a different kind of nose or different shade of skin. Perhaps you don't like your hair or your eyes or the braces or glasses you have to wear. Maybe you worry about wearing clothes that are unfashionable.

All of these worries usually arise from the same thing: a desire to be accepted. People who look good according to the world's standards seem to be happier and have more friends. You may think, *If only I looked like her, then I could be happy,* or, *If I had his cool clothes, I'd have more friends and feel important.*

Find the ANTIDOTE

Read 1 Samuel 16:7. People may notice the outside, but what does this verse tell us that God notices?

_____

_____

At times, we do judge others based on their appearance. (You can probably think of a time when you have done this!) The verse you just read comes from a true story where the prophet Samuel was choosing Israel's next king.

God had told him that the new king was one of Jesse's sons. Starting with the oldest and most impressive, Eliab, Samuel evaluated seven of Jesse's eight sons. But God hadn't chosen any of them. Finally, Samuel asked Jesse to call in his youngest son, David, from tending the sheep. Even though David was just a young boy, God saw his heart and helped Samuel understand that he was the best choice for king.

When you begin to worry about how you look, remember that God made you, thinks you are important, and sees what really matters—your heart.

The *More* Monster

The PROBLEM: I want more and more.

Do you ever wish everything in life was like an all-you-can-eat buffet? You know, the kind with pizza, mashed potatoes, garlic bread, soup, macaroni and cheese, ice cream, and a hundred other items?

What if you could walk through the toy store and pick out as many toys as you wanted for one small price? Not only that, but you could go back anytime to get more. Life would seem pretty great, don't you think?

Instead, if you're like most people, you probably feel like you never have everything you want. Even movie stars and professional athletes, who make millions of dollars a year, seem to always want more. *More, more, more.*

When you see friends enjoying their brand new clothes or the latest toy or video game, you may think that more stuff would make you happier. But that's just not the truth.

A king named Solomon, one of the wisest men to ever live, wrote a book of the Bible called Ecclesiastes. In it, he wrote these words: "Anyone who loves money never has enough. Anyone who loves wealth is never satisfied with what he gets" (Ecclesiastes 5:10 NIrV).

King Solomon had a lot of cool stuff! He had a beautiful palace. He had gold and silver. He had the finest clothes and the fastest horses and chariots. And yet, he says that no matter how much you have, it never feels like enough.

Find the ANTIDOTE

Read Matthew 6:33 and write the verse in your own words:

_____

_____

_____

The only way to avoid the "more monster" and be truly happy with what you have is to want more of the things God wants for you. Things like love, peace, joy…and other fruits of the Spirit. When you seek those things first, God will provide everything you truly need. It may not be an all-you-can-eat buffet of the stuff you desire, but it will fill you up and give you lasting joy.

EXTRA SNOOPiNG: Find out more about the fruit of the Spirit in Galatians 5:22-26!

Have Patience

PROBLEM: I have trouble waiting.

Have you ever gone to an amusement park and had to wait in a long line for a super-duper fun ride? I'm sure you wished you could just be magically transported to the front of the line and ride as many times as you wanted.

Lots of things in life require waiting. When there's a toy you really want, you may have to wait until you've saved enough of your allowance to buy it. At school, you have to raise your hand and wait for the teacher to call on you. And you have to wait for special events, such as your birthday or Christmas.

Waiting isn't always fun, and it's definitely not easy. We like to have what we want right away. But someone who develops patience—or the ability to wait—will discover big rewards.

Find the ANTIDOTE

Read Proverbs 14:29 and write down the meanings of "understanding" and "folly."

Understanding:

_____

Folly:

_____

Having patience pays off. Sometimes you may not understand the full situation until you wait to see what happens. For example, you may feel frustrated that your mom is asking you to clean your room instead of allowing you to play, but you don't know she's planning to take you to the movies later.

And some things are *worth* the wait. If you always rush into what you can get right away, you'll miss out on things that require patience to attain. Think of this: If you always spend your allowance on candy and little toys, you'll never be able to save for the bigger, more expensive toy you really want.

Sometimes waiting will still be difficult. While you wait, focus on the things you're hoping for and find useful things to spend your time doing.

When I'm waiting for something, I like to floss my teeth.

That's, um...healthy.

Help My Unbelief

The PROBLEM: I have doubts about God.

The Bible talks about a man who had a terrible problem. An evil spirit lived inside his son. The boy could not talk and sometimes the spirit inside him tried to throw him into the fire or the water to kill him.

When the man brought his son to Jesus to be healed, Jesus told him that anything was possible for the one who believed.

The man said, "I do believe; help me overcome my unbelief!"

In our world today, you will hear about many different kinds of beliefs. Some people don't believe God exists. Others believe that each person is his own god. The Bible tells us about the one true God, but that doesn't mean it's always easy to believe in Him.

Feeling uncertain about whether God is real or His Word is true is called *doubt*.

Find the ANTIDOTE

Read Proverbs 3:5-8. What does this verse tell us about getting through doubts?

_____

_____

_____

Doubt is a natural part of life. In moments of doubt, we can ask God to confirm His truth in our hearts. Here are a few ways to deal with doubt:

Don't be surprised. The Bible tells us that God's understanding and knowledge are much greater than our own. Just because we don't understand something doesn't mean it isn't true. We don't have to fear doubt, either. If the Bible is true, it can stand up to all of our questions.

Work through your doubt. Like the man in the story, we can ask God to help us believe in Him—even when we have tough questions. Jesus cast the spirit out of the man's son! Ask God to reveal answers to you through His Word or other people.

Don't do it alone. If you're experiencing doubt, talk to someone about it. Christians are meant to help each other! Maybe you're not the one having the doubts, but a friend is. Take time to talk with him or pray with him. Jude 22 says, "Be merciful to those who doubt."

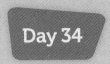

Family Troubles

The PROBLEM: My family is having problems.

Madison watched the TV screen. A happy, smiling family with a fluffy dog hugged on-screen. In the commercial, their favorite pizza had brought them together. Madison sighed. *I wish that was my family,* she thought.

Instead, Madison's dad worked long hours at the office and was hardly ever home. Her mom seemed stressed out and didn't smile much. And her older brother and sister were too busy hanging out with their friends to take time for eating pizza together, let alone a big family group-hug.

Sometimes we may feel like things aren't going well with our families. Many times these "problems" are hidden from others. It can be worrying and painful to watch an older sibling make poor decisions or to see parents fight. But whatever problems your family is facing, God is bigger.

Find the ANTIDOTE

Read Isaiah 43:2. What is God's promise to His children about going through hard times?

_____

_____

Did you know that there was no perfect family in the Bible? Think about it. Cain killed his brother Abel. Joseph got sold into slavery by his jealous brothers. And Rebekah helped her son Jacob deceive his father, Isaac. Families have been having problems since the beginning of time!

And, unfortunately, you can't fix your family's problems; only God can do that. If you're part of the problem (for example, you pull your sister's hair every day, so she's going bald) you can confess that to God and choose to be more loving in the future. But a lot of family problems will be outside of your control. In those times, God promises to be with you. Not only that, but you can ask Him to provide a solution for the problems your family is facing. He loves them even more than you do!

A problem my family is having that I want to pray about is...

_____

_____

_____

If You're Saved and You Know It

The PROBLEM: I don't know if I'm saved.

Aiden fiddled with the salt shaker on the table. "What are you thinking about?" Mom asked, sitting down next to him.

Aiden hesitated. He felt embarrassed to tell his mom what was on his mind. Aiden wasn't sure he was a Christian. He remembered saying a prayer to ask Jesus into his heart when he was really little, but last week at church, as his pastor explained more about what it meant to trust in Jesus for the forgiveness of sins, Aiden wondered if he'd ever really made that decision.

"Mom, what should I do if I'm not sure I'm a Christian?" Aiden asked. He explained how the pastor's message had made him question his salvation.

"Well, Jesus promises He'll never leave you," Mom reminded him gently, "but you can always tell Him again that you believe in Him and trust Him to be your Savior."

Aiden nodded his head. "I want to do that."

Find the ANTIDOTE

Read Acts 16:31.

What does this verse say will happen to you?

When does it say it will happen?

This verse says that you will be saved when you believe on the Lord Jesus. It is called a "condition and promise" verse—if you do something there will be a specific result.

EXTRA SNOOPING: Check out these other "condition and promise" verses and fill in the chart.

Verse	What does God ask us to do?	What does God promise?
John 1:12		
Romans 10:13		
John 3:16		

Verses like these remind us that our salvation is secure. But if you accepted Jesus as your Savior when you were really young, you may understand more about Him now. That's awesome! And if your new knowledge leads you to want to tell Him again that you believe, go right ahead.

In Hebrews 13:5 Jesus promises, "Never will I leave you; never will I forsake you." Your sin can't make you lose your salvation. If you do sin, the Bible says to tell God about what you did—just like you would a friend—to make things right between the two of you (1 John 1:9). God's salvation is complete and secure, and nothing can steal you away from Him.

Forgive and Forget

The PROBLEM: I need to forgive.

Every time Andrew thought about his ex-friend, Micah, he got an uncomfortable feeling in his chest. Andrew and Micah had been best buddies. That was until Micah made a joke about Andrew's height in front of some other guys.

Later Micah had tried to apologize, but Andrew felt too hurt to forgive. So the two quit talking and hanging out. And even though Andrew wanted to forget about what Micah had done, it was all he could think about. *What kind of friend says such mean things?* Andrew thought. *If our friendship was real, he wouldn't have embarrassed me in front of everyone.*

Andrew expected the bad feelings would eventually go away, but with each passing day they seemed to get worse. Andrew was stuck in unforgiveness, and it was making him miserable.

Find the ANTIDOTE

Read Colossians 3:13. List one reason we should forgive others:

_____

_____

A famous Christian writer named C.S. Lewis (who wrote the Chronicles of Narnia) said: "To be a Christian means to forgive the inexcusable because God has forgiven the inexcusable in you." The best way to forgive someone is to remember all of the things God has forgiven you for.

Maybe you think, *I've never done something as bad as that person.* Maybe not, but the Bible says everyone has sinned and fallen short of God's standard. That means everyone needs forgiveness. And when we fail to forgive another person, it shows that we don't really value God's forgiveness in our own lives.

EXTRA SNOOPING: Look up Romans 3:23.

Forgiving someone frees your heart and mind to love God and other people instead of holding a grudge. If you need help forgiving, try these tips:

Pray. Thank God that He has forgiven you and ask Him for help to forgive the other person.

Talk. If a friend has apologized, tell her that you forgive her and make things right.

Forget. You may never totally forget how someone hurt you, but once you have forgiven, refuse to spend time thinking about it. First Corinthians 13 says that love "keeps no record of wrongs."

I Promise...Maybe

The PROBLEM: I didn't keep my promise.

Have you ever made a promise that later seemed impossible to keep?

Maybe you told a friend you would keep a secret, but you let it slip out to someone else. You may have promised that you would help your sister with a project, but then something else came up and you had to back out. Or maybe you promised your parents you wouldn't do something again (like fight with your brother), but in a moment of weakness you did.

Someone has said: "It's easy to make promises—it's hard work to keep them." Unfortunately, everyone will break a promise at some time. Does that mean we shouldn't make any promises, just in case we can't keep them? Check out what the Bible has to say.

Find the ANTIDOTE

Read the following verses and answer the questions.

Psalm 15:1-4. If you have made a promise, what should you try to do?

_____

_____

Ecclesiastes 5:5. Sometimes there is a different solution that happens before you ever make the promise. What is it?

_____

_____

A person who keeps her promises is someone who can be trusted. If you make a promise, it's important to do everything you can to keep it (unless you are keeping a secret for a friend that an adult needs to know about—then it's okay to tell).

Another part of being someone people can trust is not making promises that are going to be difficult to keep. The Bible says, "All you need to say is simply 'Yes' or 'No'; anything beyond this comes from the evil one" (Matthew 5:37). Even though it feels good to make promises, Satan can use broken promises to drive wedges between friends and ruin reputations.

So keep it simple: Before you make a promise, ask yourself and God if you are going to be able to keep it. If the answer is yes, say "yes" and then do what you said you would.

Day 38

Unfriended

The PROBLEM: I don't have any friends.

Pal. Buddy. BFF. There are lots of words for friends.

But while some people seem to have lots of friends and make new ones easily, others may not even have one good friend. Maybe you're part of the second group and feel like you don't have any friends. Not having a good buddy can feel really lonely.

That's because God created us to have relationships with other people, and friends are a big part of that. The right kind of friend can make you laugh, give you good advice, and encourage you when you're having a problem. And you don't need lots of friends to be happy. Even one or two really good pals can make a difference.

Find the ANTIDOTE

Read Proverbs 17:17. According to this verse, what does a friend do?

_____

_____

The first step to making the right kind of friend is being the right kind of friend. When you are kind, friendly, and take an interest in what others have to say, people are more likely to be attracted to you and want to strike up a friendship. Check out some other qualities you should look for in a friend.

83

EXTRA SNOOPING: Look up these verses and write down the quality of a friend you find in each.

Proverbs 13:20

_____

Proverbs 18:24

_____

Proverbs 27:17

_____

Make a list of some of the qualities you've appreciated about friends you've had in the past:

_____

_____

　　Are you striving to have those same qualities in your inter-actions with others? Remember that Jesus is your best friend and ask Him to provide you with the right kind of pals—friends you can have fun with who will also strengthen your faith.

You're my best friend, Burt.

Thanks, Squirt. I'm touched.

Well, it was either you or Astrid, my lizard.

Thanks a Lot!

The PROBLEM: I don't feel thankful.

Jake didn't feel thankful. He had to share a room with his little brother. He didn't get his own cell phone like his best friend, Manny. And he wasn't even allowed to watch TV on weeknights. All Jake could think about were the things he *didn't* have.

He didn't stop to think about how fortunate he was to have a warm, safe house to live in, a mom who made sure he had dinner every night, and parents who cared about him enough to make rules.

Sometimes our desire for things we don't have can make us feel like life is pretty bad, when in reality, we have *a lot* to be thankful for!

Find the ANTIDOTE

Read 1 Thessalonians 5:16-18. In which of the situations listed below should you be thankful? (Circle the correct answer.)

A. Your dog is lost.

B. You get an A on your math test.

C. You have to clean your room.

D. Your grandparents are coming to visit.

E. You receive $50.

F. All of the above

Did you answer F? Okay, so that was kind of a trick question. The Bible says to give thanks in ALL circumstances because it's God's will for you. That doesn't mean that you have to be happy that your bike is broken or your dog ran away. It just means that you can always find *something* to be thankful for. (And probably many things!)

When you quit focusing on the things you don't have and turn your attention to all that you do have, it reminds you Who is really in charge of your life—God. Even if you have nothing else, you can be thankful that He sent His Son to die for you so that you could have your sins forgiven. It's hard to complain about your life when you think about that amazing gift.

Take a few minutes to make a list of some of the things you are thankful for. Then give thanks to God for the awesome things He's done for you!

_____

_____

_____

God, Are You There?

The PROBLEM: I don't know how to talk to God.

Henry loved to talk. He could talk about anything to anyone at any time. He talked to his dad. He talked to his coach. He talked to his best friend. He even talked to his dog.

But when it came to talking to God, Henry got silent. He clammed up. He had *no* idea what to say.

It can feel a little strange to talk to Someone who doesn't talk back (at least not out loud). Talking to God is called *prayer*, and it's a very important part of a Christian's life. But making prayer a regular part of your life can take a little practice.

Find the ANTIDOTE

Read 1 John 5:14-15. What is the reason we can be confident when we talk to God and ask Him for things?

_____

_____

_____

There are many different things you can talk to God about. You can confess your sins (1 John 1:9), make requests (Philippians 4:6), ask for wisdom (James 1:5) and thank Him (1 Corinthians 1:4). Even Jesus's closest friends—the disciples—didn't know how to talk to God. Jesus gave them an example of how they should pray in what is called the "Lord's Prayer."

EXTRA SNOOPING: Read the Lord's Prayer in Matthew 6:9-13.

Once you know what to talk to God about, decide on a good time to pray. Maybe you already pray before meals and bedtime. That's a great start! But 1 Thessalonians 5:17 takes it a step further, saying, "Pray continually." You can talk to God any time of the day about anything. And the cool part is, He promises to hear you and answer!

Congratulations! You snooped through all of the devotions in this book and found LOTS of answers from God's Word.

Remember—
I'm a Truth Sleuth,
Squirt's a Truth Sleuth,
and you can be
a Truth Sleuth too!

Truth Sleuth Log

You're reading a lot of promises in God's Holy Word, the Bible. Sometimes you'll find a verse that has an extra special meaning for you or seems especially important because of a problem you have. When you find those verses, write them down here so you can come back and remember them later!

Where I Found It (book, chapter, and verse)	What It Says	Date

Where I Found It (book, chapter, and verse)	What It Says	Date

Where I Found It (book, chapter, and verse)	What It Says	Date

Where I Found It (book, chapter, and verse)	What It Says	Date

Where I Found It (book, chapter, and verse)	What It Says	Date

Where I Found It (book, chapter, and verse)	What It Says	Date

Jon Nappa is an award-winning writer. His works have been featured on PBS, TLC, Hallmark, and other networks, and his historical fiction novels, *Storm Warriors* and *Storm Survivors*, resulted in the founding of Storm Warriors International, a not-for-profit organization producing inspirational media supporting humanitarian causes around the globe. You can learn about his projects at stormwarriors.org and thesupersnoopers.com.

Suzanne Hadley Gosselin lives in Colorado with her husband, Kevin, and three children. Formerly an editor for *Clubhouse* and *Clubhouse Jr.* magazines, she has written for Zondervan, David C. Cook, and Focus on the Family. Suzanne enjoys sharing a good cup of coffee and conversation with a friend, serving with her husband in children's ministry, and visiting her family in the Pacific Northwest.

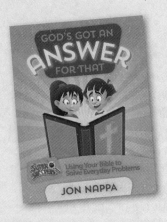

God's Got an Answer for That!

God's Talking to *Me?*

Every kid has problems...and they can feel overwhelming.

* "I don't want to forgive my brother, but Mom says I have to."
* "I don't want to go to bed on time."
* "I'm being bullied, and I'm not sure who I can talk to."
* "I cheated on a test, and now I feel so guilty."
* "I'm lonely, and I don't have any friends."

God doesn't have anything to say about *those* problems, does He? You'd be surprised! When you open God's Word, you'll find answers to all sorts of real-life questions. Discover how reading the Bible can help you every day!